© Copyright 2017 by CiJiRO Publishing
- All rights reserved.

This document is geared toward providing exact and reliable information in regard to the topic and issue covered. The publication is sold with the idea that the publisher is not required to render accounting, officially permitted, or otherwise, qualified services. If advice is necessary, legal or professional, a practiced individual in the profession should be ordered.

- From a Declaration of Principles which was accepted and approved equally by a Committee of the American Bar Association and a Committee of Publishers and Associations.

In no way is it legal to reproduce, duplicate, or transmit any part of this document in either electronic means or in printed format. Recording of this publication is strictly prohibited and any storage of this document is not allowed unless with written permission from the publisher. All rights reserved.

The information provided herein is stated to be truthful and consistent, in that any liability, in terms of inattention or otherwise, by any usage or abuse of any policies, processes, or directions contained within is the solitary and utter responsibility of the recipient reader. Under no circumstances will any legal responsibility or blame be held against the publisher for any reparation, damages, or monetary loss due to the information herein, either directly or indirectly.

Respective authors own all copyrights not held by the publisher.

The information herein is offered for informational purposes solely, and is universal as so. The presentation of the information is without contract or any type of guarantee assurance.

The trademarks that are used are without any consent, and the publication of the trademark is without permission or backing by the trademark owner. All trademarks and brands within this book are for clarifying purposes only and are the owned by the owners themselves, not affiliated with this document.

RAISING BEEF CATTLE FOR BEGINNERS

Table of Contents

CHAPTER 1 11
   Introduction 11
CHAPTER 2 15
   Starting your herd 15
   How much land do you have at your disposal? 19
   How many cows can you realistically have on your acreage? 21
   Climate and temperature where you live 24
   Finding good animals to start with 26
   Popular breeds for beef cattle 27
Chapter 3 37
   Setting up your farm for beef cattle 37
   Food and water 40
   How much forage is on your land 42
   Supplementary feeding- Hay and corn/grain 44
      Grain 45
      Hay 45
   Disadvantage of corn/grain over hay and grass consumption 46

Times of the year for pasturing and supplementary feeding 47

Water for cattle and winter tank heaters for water flow 48

Algae growth 50

CHAPTER 4 52

Maintaining Your Herd 53

Common Cattle Diseases and Preventions .. 53

Clostridial Diseases 54

Respiratory disease (pneumonia) stress .. 60

Deworming 75

Finding a good vet 75

CHAPTER 5 77

Harvesting 77

How To Find A Slaughter House/Packer 78

Getting The Meat Processed For Sale 78

Joining And Selling The Processed Meat To A Farm Coorpeative 79

CHAPTER 6 81

Selling Your Cattle 81

Selling during the springs 81

Selling during fall 82

Selling bulls, calves, cows. Which are the best to sell?..83

Selling to your neighbors and others in your local community 83

Selling at livestock auctions 84

CONCLUSION 86

Great articles, videos, and more!

- Homesteading
- Ranching
- Farming
- Self-Sustainability
- Working for yourself
- Living a Fulfilling, Stress-Free Life!

Visit:

www.FunHappyLives.com

CHAPTER 1

Introduction

Humans love meat which is great because it is an essential protein that is required by the body for muscle and bone building. Even some experts go ahead to say that beef contain fats that can protect the heart from diseases.

Expert studies also show that beef (especially from grass-fed cattle) secrete acids which limits the risk of diabetes and cancer and also build up a person's immune system against other diseases in the body.

Raising beef cattle will prove to be an amazing journey for beginners who commit to it. There are thousands of reasons why you should raise your own head of cattle but none trump the fact that you would have bought yourself a first class ticket to an endless supply of nutritious meats and steaks.

Even more, because of the imperative demand for rich meat, beef cattle rearing would make for good money making venture. There are several modes to turn beef cattle rearing into a business, one can make a living from it and literarily enjoy the fruits of his labor at the same time as well.

Whatever you may choose to do with your beef cattle, they must be properly nurtured and cared for to ensure that they get to the height of what they can be and produce to a maximum of their capacity.

From their housing arrangements to feeding plan, every detail must be greatly considered and satisfied for optimal results in the success of your beef cattle adventure.

CHAPTER 2

Starting your herd

It is important to get it right from the start and iron out every single detail from the beginning stages of your farm or ranch. This can make all the difference if your operation is bound to be a great success or a colossal failure

In starting a beef cattle operation, what is needed is a farm or a ranch where you are able to nurture and raise your beef cattle to be grown for that high demand beef. It should be noted that calves that are raised to become beefers comes from two different ways. There is the commercial way and then there is the seed stock.

What is the commercial way? The commercial way is the most popularly chosen method amongst beginners mainly because it is easier to get a grasp of it than of the seed stock operation. In commercial breeding, the farmer is expected to acquire crossbred cows (sometimes the entire herd may be of the same breed), then feed and raise them solely for the purpose of beef production. As earlier stated, most beginner ranchers would prefer this method of operation to start with, because of the ease of operation, while they gain the experience in cattle rearing.

Seed stock is a direct kind of way that is almost only practiced by expert long-term cattle ranchers. In seed stocking the rancher chooses to go with a specific kind of breed (could be more than one kind) and sell them out to cattle producers as replacement stock. This is where it gets tricky for the rookies because unlike the cattle rearing veterans, newbies have no idea which cattle is best for their local area and other very vital information such as what crossbreeding combinations are the best to accomplish the ideal calf..

In a nutshell beginners best start off with commercial raising operations for the purposes of beef, where they can easily find their way around, obtaining meaningful experience and necessary knowledge building about all-things cattle raising and they can then later go on to seed stock operation at the point when they have become familiar with the ins and outs of the cattle raising business.

When you have decided on which cattle rearing operation to indulge in, you can move straight on to the planning stage in which you should determine what things there are to do, and how you should set out to accomplish them. Your planning stages should be well thought out and should encompass every detail of your newly upstarting beef cattle ranching business from herd acquisition to financial details, as well as day to day management of operations.

At this stage it should be wise to create a spreadsheet to make it easier to keep track of all important information. There are a lot of various factors to consider that would be determinants to whether or not your beef cattle raising project would thrive.

For example not every breed would do well under your geographical zone. Some breeds might perform very favorably where you set them up and at the same time others might prove too high a cost to maintain, not because they are generally expensive to maintain but because of their adaptability to the climate of your area.

Be sure research in trade publications and meet other local ranchers in your area to learn important information essential to your local area as well as other factors so you can keep up on the latest information that can be beneficial to your cattle. The internet could be a wild card sometimes but at the same time there is vital information that could be difficult to dig out elsewhere which you might only find through the internet.

Browse for reliable cattle sources online and cross-reference them.

Visit veterans in the business and learn religiously if they would let you. Believe me learning from an expert is far better than learning from anywhere on the internet or learning from the pages of any pasture staining book.

Inquire about anything that might be useful or that is related to beef cattle rearing business from breeding to weaning, feeding to reproduction, body condition and environmental effect on specific breeds. Learn every single thing that comes to mind in regards to cattle rearing. You would be doing yourself a whole lot of good to do some heavy research.

How much land do you have at your disposal?

There are basic things that are needed for cattle rearing and one of such basic things is land. Obviously without land, there is no ranch or farm. How else would you raise your herd?

That being said, you shouldn't simply just walk up to any land seller and acquire his or her land to build up your ranch or farm. There might be limiting factors that could make some certain lands uncomfortable and unsuitable for beef cattle rearing.

To get it right in terms of land, you must keep in mind the number of cows per acre of land bearing in mind other things that would be sited in the farm from the building structures in the farm to the machineries that would need to be situated in it.

It becomes a question of how much land your cattle need. Obviously you would not even consider raising beef cattle if you live in a tight place and do not have the means of acquiring a decently large piece of land.

There are not any rules written in stone that spells out rightly the size of ranch that you would need for your cattle farming purposes, but there are general ideas from which you could derive an approximate measurement of acreage which would be suitable for your herd.

How much land you need also rests on the shoulders of other factors such as if you plan on grazing your herd all season and all year round. It also depends on if you plan to confine them to a paddock or not.

It depends on the type of climate in your area. Will your cattle remain able to graze even when the skies begin to rain down ice? Bearing in mind that grazing is perhaps the most important task in the life of a cow, they go as long as eating for as much as 12 hours every day and there need to be constant supply of pasture.

The fact is that you can never really be as certain of how much land you really need. There may or may not be 'getting it right' but there definitely is 'getting it wrong', so it is best that you obtain only as many cows as your land can aptly contain. To make up for the shortfall, you can always do supplement grazing with hay if need be.

How many cows can you realistically have on your acreage?

After you have settled the issue of land, your new term of preference becomes the number of cows you have on your acreage.

Where some beginners usually get it wrong in assuming one cow per acre and completely turning their back on other factors.

There are several other factors that should also play a part in your decision in the whole thing.

There is the issue of location and by that I do not mean your country or state alone but a more precise location. Pinpoint the area you are in and look out for variations with other places.

If you think that your soil type does not have anything whatsoever to do with your whole ranch plan, then you couldn't be more wrong. Remember that the food quality that you provide your herd is everything when it comes to rearing cattle, and the soil itself has direct impact on the quality of pasture that becomes available to your cattle.

A weak soil therefore becomes tantamount to insufficient nutrients for your cattle just as quality soil would mean high nutrients and more forage quantity for your ranch.

Now talking about forage quality in your ranch as to how it has direct impact on the number of cattle that an acre can comfortably contain, the rule is that the more forage yield you have, the more cattle you become able to place in an acre of land. Of course the quality and quantity of it varies at different time of the year, so you must bear in mind that once the quantity and or quality of the vegetation dwindles at a certain point in time, be sure the number of cows you have per that acre.

Beef cattle unlike its dairy counterpart tends to consume lesser pasture, hence an ideal beef cattle ranch or farm manages to contain more cattle per acre than a dairy cattle farm.

Also you should consider the class of your cattle when figuring out the cattle per acre mathematics. Take into account their age and gender, and consider their weights in pounds or kilograms as it is an imperative factor in the cattle per acre rule. When you have animals of varying sizes, and you always do, the larger ones tend to consume more pasture than the smaller ones hence the need arises for such animals to be provided greater areas of land to graze.

You might have heard of carrying capacity for roads and buildings. Well it is similar to what we are talking about here also. The carrying capacity of a land in terms of beef cattle raising becomes the number of beef cattle that can be placed on the land for a whole season without causing any damage to its primary features in form of overgrazing or otherwise. Whether the issue is overgrazing or under grazing, it should be treated with care as such deficiency or over efficiency might have damaging effects to the soil.

All these guidelines do not give you exactly how many cattle you should place per acre but it does gives you an idea of what to do.

Climate and temperature where you live

When it comes to weather and climate impacts on beef cattle, it becomes a bit unpredictable and this has its way of tampering with the balance of management.

It is a given that some certain stress factors as a result of overcrowding, air pollution, etc will succeed in having negative impact on your beef cattle. Whether or not beef cattle would perform at their optimal level might just be up to the climate and temperature condition you live in.

For starters, the chance of reproduction activities within your herd becomes negatively affected by high temperatures. Newborn and young calves on their own might not survive a serious cold weather spell because of small amount of its insulative tissue. And although at extremes, both weather conditions become seriously detrimental. There is an increase in mortality during the cold periods.

How the climate and temperature are in your area is is a question you should answer before you set up your ranch at all. Do you stay in an area where there is extreme cold or heat or mild cold or heat?

If you stay in an area that meets the average weather requirements, then the need for a special type of shelter or shade shouldn't even come into question. However for areas with chilling wind, provide shelters for calves as such winds can be highly detrimental to them.

Be sure to provide a heating or cooling system for your shelter as the case may be. Planting trees does its own job acting as shade for your animals.

Windbreaks also can do a lot of good in areas of cold conditions.

Enclosed shelter might not sit well with the animals but it is really for their own good. Experts say that moderate and or cold weather system has little or no impact on cattle but heat or severe cold will definitely leave its bad mark.

Finding good animals to start with

Finding the right animals that are adapted for your climate and area becomes necessary for those who seek to succeed in this business. You can easily get any type of beef cattle and stock your farm with them, only this way you have made your farm susceptible to heavy loss.

There are several types of very good beef cattle but it becomes a bit hard to know which one would be a good fit for your farm especially as a beginner.

The key is starting off with a few cows and seeing how well they would fare. And while you are at it, acquire cows that have good temperament and forage convertibility.

So now it is well established that different cattle breeds are best suited to different climate conditions and different environment and as such even a less popular breed might end up becoming what is best for your stock because of the area where you live.

So when seeking the best fit for your farm or cattle ranch, you might want to go for the minor breeds or crossbreeds for chances that they best adapt to your climate and area.

Popular breeds for beef cattle

As the name implies, beef cattle is ultimately reared for beef production and so it becomes only wise that the farmer targets to get his animal to the largest size and greatest strength that the cattle can attain.

Let us take a look at some breeds that are known to yield high in terms of beef production:

Black Angus

The Angus would more than likely top any chart of beef cattle production as it stands as the most popular breed in the United States, and in the year 2014, the British cattle movement service named it the UK's Most popular native beef breed and second most popular breed overall. They are amazingly hardy and thrive even under very cold and harsh weather conditions. The average weight of bulls is about 2,000 lbs, while an average cow is around 1,150 lbs. The Black Angus breed are naturally polled and black in color.

They are a lot of farmers' favorite also as a result of their ability of overcoming dystocia (birthing problems) which makes them a popular choice for crossbreeding.

With Angus you get their full worth for pasture consumed as they efficiently convert them into body weight which means more beef.

Herefordshire

If there were no Angus, the Herefordshire cattle would be a first recommendation to beef cattle farmers especially beginners because of their great ability to adapt to various climates and areas.

They are most often less pricey to acquire when compared to the Angus but still utilizes pasture to obtain a great body weight almost as good of a ratio as the Angus.

They come between 1200 to 1800 pounds and are capable of living for up to 13 years. The females live longer than the males and can live for as long as 15 years.

They are docile; they mature early and prove to be a great money making meat investment.

Limousin

Yet another popular beef cattle breed, the Limousin cattle originates from somewhere in France. They are known for their rare ease in ability to adapt to harsh climate and rugged terrain and also their good health., What's even better is that the Limousin is not only just another beef cattle but it is also known to be a work animal, which is a bonus point from the point of view of the farmer or rancher.

Their reproductive prowess is excellent, thereby raking in more money for breeders. They are a strong and muscled cattle that have the ability to convert pasture to lean tender meat.

This hardy animal is most favorably crossbred with Angus or Hereford.

Gelbvieh

This is an all-purpose breed cattle that originates from Germany. By all-purpose I mean that it is reared for the production of good beef, milk and that it is also a work animal. They are mostly found in black colors lately and are found to be between 1600 lbs and 2200 lbs. They are also another hardy breed known for the ability to overcome harsh weather conditions and cold temperature. They also easily adapt to different environments.

They have very heavy muscle, good temperament and are quite the friendly type to have around the farm or ranch.

The Gelbvieh breed have good reproductive prowess and turn out to be great mothers coupled with their ability to produce plenty of milk. They require clean water and enough pasture to convert to high quality meat.

Fun Fact: did you know that the Gelbvieh cattle can hear high and low frequencies better than humans can? Now you know.

Wagyu

This pretty big bag of meat originates from Japan. They are known for their easy birthing, fitness, lack of excess back fat and their fertility.

They have good temperament and are very easy to handle. They also very easily adapt to different environments and climatic conditions.

This hardy variety comes in four breeds: Japanese brown, Japanese black, Japanese polled and Japanese shorthorn.

Chapter 3

Setting up your farm for beef cattle

Setting up your farm for beef cattle might turn out to be a no brainer only if you move in the right direction.

Alright the dream begins with acquiring a couple acres of land if you don't have any, and then acquiring the right animals to stock in your farm. Simple right? Maybe, but then it could get tricky if you don't follow the right steps. Where to begin from now?

- One thing that is important is ensuring that your intention to work in beef cattle raising comes with a bit of passion to say the least or start off as a dream for you.

  Of course it doesn't need to be that prominent childhood dream but it should at least be something that you think about a bit more frequently. Basically, you will learn to love it for the beauty of nature and getting closer to your family, even though you are probably in it for the money.

If you do not find a way to build up your interest and you embark on the journey anyway, then you might be in for a bumpy ride.

- Armed with passion or what may seem like it, you must be prepared to part ways with your hard earned money. If you see that you probably do not have enough of it to get started, then you might want to consider partnering up with someone with similar goals.

If you have got a spouse that is somewhat sound financially, you should capitalize on it. Sell your Idea in a creative way and make him or her fall in love with it enough to acquire a couple of calves and a farmland immediately.

- Even though you might manage to get a partner, your combined money might still not be enough to start up with several cattle and a large farmstead. Instead of waiting to grow your money to be that big, start small as your money would carry. Buy a couple of calves and acquire a land big enough to conveniently contain your cattle. If you can't immediately buy such land, then get a lease with a plan to buy the land or some other land in the future.

- Do not quit your regular job at least just yet. At the early stage, your farm would probably give you little or nothing of a profit. In fact most new cattle farms run on deficit at such early stages especially when they are being operated by rookies.
- Fencing and safety is a priority for your farmstead. Consider setting up an electric fence to keep your cattle within the space provided for them and also to keep predators at bay. Add value to your farm from time to time, doing some real cleanup and replacing obsolete items.
- Get short term and long term loans but mostly short term loans at the

early stages of things and then expand later. Buy up neighboring farms that may become available with big prospects and continue to grow your herd with more cows.
- Do not be so quick to acquire heavy machineries. You can make do with the little you have and improvise where the need be later on. Often times, obtaining necessary used but reliable equipment, is a good way to save costs over new equipment when starting up.
- Plant grasses that thrive and contain high nutrients that your herd need.

Food and water

After land and the cattle themselves, food and water are the most important things that should be settled on as to regards for beef cattle rearing.

In beef cattle rearing, you must ensure that the food and the water sources are conveniently settled even before you acquire your calves.

Studies have shown that in producing a pound of beef, about 1800 gallons water is expended during the lifetime of the animal.

The good thing about cattle feeding is that it goes down in cost as your herd grows.

Real planning and analysis are required if you are to succeed in these regards. You must determine how much water and feed would be required to get your cow to a marketable standard.

For cattle to attain a reasonable weight when due, it must be properly fed with the correct ration of food. For example the food must contain at least 11 percent of protein that comprises wheat, and corn or barley.

Adequate amount of forage would improve the weight of cattle to a great extent. Your feeding strategy should be flexible as grain prices tends to fluctuate.

How much forage is on your land

A very good question would be how much forage your land contains? And then how much forage does a cow really need?

Forage can be expensive sometimes and so cattle farmers get a close estimate of how much of it their animals need per day to provide necessary nutrients that they need.

Several factors determine a cow's daily forage intake: the weight of the cow and the stage of production are principal determining factors.

It is only logical that cows that weight more tend to consume more then cows that weigh less. In that vein, cows that are in the stages of gestation also require more forage than the ones that are not.

The quality of forage that is available to the herd also play its own role in the scheme of things. Just as humans would prefer good food, if the quality of the forage is high (that is when it contains more leaf than stem), the cattle would consume more of it but when the quality is low (when it contains more stem than leaf), the appetite of the cows tend to reduce and then they leave most of it unattended to.

According to Rick Rosloy, a beef specialist in the University of Nebraska, some rules of thumb can be used to determine the daily intake of food by cows.

When the forage quality is low and the cow is not in the period of gestation, they would eat up as much as 1.8 percent of their weight while those in gestation period eat up as much as 2 percent of their weight.

So determining the amount of food that a cow takes in a day would give you the basis for which to know the amount of forage that is required to be in your farm.

However, during a drought, farmers record a low amount of forage but they take inventory to determine the amount of supplement they would need.

Supplementary feeding- Hay and corn/grain

During periods of extreme weather conditions, you may not have it as good as you did when the weather was fair. This is especially in regards to cow feed (grasses) primarily during the winter period.

The grasses in which your cattle feed on become redundant and inconsumable thus forcing you to stockpile alternative feeds throughout the duration of the winter. A smart farmer would even make such provision much earlier for his herd because when winter comes, such commodities becomes scarce and the prices of it skyrocket in the market.

Failure to make such provisions would probably force the farmer to take drastic measure such as selling off the cows. Some farmers do recommend the use of Nitrogen fertilizer during such period but the question remains, how effective is it?

To me and a whole lot of other farmers,, the best choice during harsh periods would be to procure additional feeders in grain and or hay.

Grain

Grains are great food supplements to provide your herd whether or not it is winter. However they should be slowly introduced into the diet of your herd as it has been observed that quick introduction of grains for cattle can ultimately cause death.

The need does arise for your grains to be crushed for better digestion causing most farmers to go for oats because of the lesser need and ease to crush.

Hay

Hay is another good supplement during the cold wet winter. In fact some would say that next to pasture, hay is the next best thing for your cows. It does come in different categories with variations in both quality and availability. There are grasses hay, legumes hay and mixed hay (combination of grass and legumes).

There is also such a thing as cereal grain and it is better when harvested while it is still growing rather than waiting up for it to mature.

Examples of some good hays are: orchard grass, blue grass, alfalfa, and others.

Disadvantage of corn/grain over hay and grass consumption

Grain is very suitable for farming but if you are stuck between two choices, it would be best that you go for hay rather than grain because of the several disadvantages of grain over hay and grass consumption in the art of cattle rearing.

One of such disadvantages is the uneasiness to transport the grains to a new location. With hay there is an easiness to transport it because of its lighter state hence translating to a reduction in the cost of transportation. With grain, the cost of transportation drastically increases as a result of dry matter basis.

With grain, the cost of delivery in regards to protein and metabolized energy is significantly higher than in the case of grain.

And while hay has more uses and market outlets, grain does have less of those uses and a higher bailing cost on the basis of dark matter.

Times of the year for pasturing and supplementary feeding

Ordinarily the non winter period is the right time for your cattle to get into the field and feed on highly nutritious grass and be merry. However industrialization over the years has changed mainstream farming behaviors for farmers to provide supplements as grain to their herd in normal grazing period as well.

Ideally, the cold wet winter period rings the bell for supplementary feed but even this notion has again been compromised by industrialization. Nowadays, farmers have found ways around this limitation by introducing the use of nitrogen fertilizers which works alright when used.

The key to knowing which time of the year your cows should feed on grass or supplementary feed as hay and grains boils down to cost effectiveness and the level of nutrients that is guaranteed per mode of feeding.

In this regard, you are to determine which feed satisfies the need for nutrients and at the same time being the most cost effective.

Water for cattle and winter tank heaters for water flow

Previously, we have established that on the average, a pound of beef requires some 1800 gallons of water. This only goes to tell us the importance of water in beef cattle production.

Again you should note that the water requirement depends on the production stage of the cattle such as its period of gestation, the current temperature, and its weight. When the weight of the cattle increases, the water demand increases too. In the same vein, when the temperature increases, so does the need for water. Animals in gestation period would require more water than animals that are not in gestation period.

Ideally, the amount of water required by the cow on a daily basis is between 5 to 30 gallons of water.

Cows in gestation period require almost twice as much as cows not in gestation.

Ensure that the water provided for your cows is free from dirt and other wastes.

Indeed maintaining a fresh supply of water for your cow might be an arduous task especially during the winter period but it is essential that you do as some cows are not used to drinking chilled water and may never be.

A good method in dealing with this problem is the introduction of winter tank heaters. In this system, water continually runs through the tank, in and out. These heaters come in different sizes depending on your demand and it requires a steady source of electricity at least during the winter period.

It does an amazing job in keeping the water above the freezing level thus keeping your animals very happy.

Algae growth

One thing that poses to be a stubborn problem especially during the hot summer time is the growth of algae in water tanks. The need for fresh and algae free water for you cows cannot be overemphasized hence the need for a way to dealing with this menace.

- Cleaning! Cleaning!! And cleaning!!! It is always the first step to dealing with any disease related problems. Regular removal of water is perhaps the most effective method in this regards and even though it is such a difficult task, is necessary as long standing water provides an easy environment for algae and some other bacteria to infiltrate the tanks.
- There are a couple of chemical products in the market that kills algae effectively. Chlorine and copper are two of such chemicals; however you much be aware of the ration of the chemicals against water before you use such chemicals.

CHAPTER 4

Maintaining Your Herd

Common Cattle Diseases and Preventions

When it comes to beef cattle, it primarily has to do with productivity which translates to big profits and diseases being slim to none in your herd. A healthy head of cattle is a happy head of cattle. It eats well, moves with grace and plays nice with her pare and make good money for her owner.

Diseases in cattle are disastrous and should be prevented by all means necessary. The truth remains that no matter the breed of cattle you keep within the four walls of your ranch, the key to healthy, happy and productive cattle is disease prevention.

Your cattle are susceptible to several diseases which becomes adamant in over populated herds no matter how slight. Stress and discomfort might also be a reason for your cattle's ailment. All in all, beef cattle fall into amongst these types of diseases:

Clostridial Diseases

Clostridial diseases are caused by Clostridial organisms which are mainly found in soils and they have quite the survival rate which makes them dangerously persistent. They may also occur naturally within the guts of the host animals and might even be as harmless as it can be and only contaminate the soil when it gets out.

Quick and correct diagnosis is crucial when it is suspected that Clostridial disease might be the cause of death in your herd.

Often times, cases of death that have been thought to be as a result of Clostridial diseases have actually turned out to be anthrax. Of course it is imperative that a cow thought to be dying of anthrax must be left undisturbed until the vet says otherwise.

Clostridial diseases on its own can be deadly disastrous and causes dark days in the life of cattle owners.

They happen on par with some not so good conditions such as blackleg and black diseases and then there is tetanus.

The very best first thing to do when there is a suspected case of Clostridial is to call for A Vet as he alone can rightly diagnose and known what step should be taken next and If the animal is right for vaccination or not.

Clostridial cases are treated with the use of antitoxins and large doses of antibiotics but these are quite costly to acquire and might not give that desired result that you seek. So what to do?

Prevention and control is a lot more convenient than a cure don't you think?

Animals have an immune system which when rightly equipped would help to fight diseases that it can very well fight. This is one big gun (probably the biggest) in the fight against Clostridial. Certainly a couple of factors have to be taken into consideration from economic factors to the likelihood of the disease, but your best bet is getting your animals immunized.

Immunization itself takes certain different stances. There comes active and passive immunizations. With passive, we talk about the transfer of resistance from mothers to their infants while active. On the other hand has to do with "actively" shooting the animal with required doses of vaccine.

Clostridial diseases come in different strains, which vary depending on location, time of the year and the weather.

Let's take a look at some of these unpleasant ailments and how they occur in cattle.

- **Blackleg**

Blackleg has been found out to mostly occur when cattle are disturbed by moving from one pasture to another entirely different one. They can also occur as a result of muscle damage.

It ultimately leads to sudden death of the animal and quick decomposition of the animal's carcass.

Blacklegs have been known to happen in areas after earth or construction works have been carried out including drainage works and road construction. The aftermath of these construction works would expose the earth to resistant Clostridial spores.

In most cases, cows that are affected by Clostridial turn lazy and depressed, lose their appetite and ultimately die.

- **Black disease**

It is believed that black disease occurs as a result of damage to the liver by migration of young liver flukes and doesn't restrict itself to a certain age of cattle; it affects all ages and ultimately causes death of the cattle.

Unfortunately there is no cure yet know for black disease so prevention and control cannot be over emphasized when dealing with it.

Black disease also known as infectious necrotic hepatitis causes plug of yellow tissue mostly on the surface of the liver and signs of damaged liver fluke are usually always obvious. The carcasses of the dead animal usually decompose very rapidly.

- **Tetanus**

Tetanus disease mostly occurs as a result of contamination of wounds and probably from the use of rings for marking and also from dog bites. They may also occur from after calving.

It produces a powerful toxin which ferociously hit hard at the nervous system of your animal. Cows that are affected by tetanus diseases shows various signs such as difficulty in walking as their legs becomes stiff and sometimes numb.

Cattle slowly respond to treatments for tetanus disease which does cause seizure after a while and can ultimately cause death.

- **Malignant Oedema**

Another disease in the Clostridial family is the malignant oedema. It is caused by different Clostridial and is popularly known to occur after contaminated intermuscular injection. It causes inflation and swelling plus great pain and discomfort to the cow which might later translate to lameness. Cattle that contract this problem usually die within 24-48 hours of contraction.

Treatment even by penicillin doesn't do so much good but vaccination of the animals usually does the trick in prevention..

- **Botulism**

This is where keeping birds around the ranch around your cattle might become detrimental. Some experts say that the most cases of botulism have been as a result of poultry mess on pasture that will afterwards be consumed by the cattle.

Spoilt poultry manure and carcasses of poultry animals top the chart of causes of cases of botulism.

It causes weakness if the muscles and hind legs at the initial stages and if recovery does not happen; it would lead to sudden death of the affected cow.

Respiratory disease (pneumonia) stress

Cattle do live together in their ranch thereby making it easy for airborne diseases to spread quickly when it is contracted by one. They are caused by some annoying little microorganism which your cattle might have picked up somewhere maybe while grazing or even just simply moving around. Respiratory diseases are always airborne - diseases that animals spread through coughing, sneezing, etc.

Some farmers believe that cattle are more susceptible to respiratory diseases mostly after transportation of new livestock probably after purchasing. Before you purchase a cow, keep in mind that it must have been at a ranch or farm with different other cattle penned together with it.

When it comes to beef cattle, two types of pneumonia exist: there is the viral type and the bacteria type. The virus always normally attack the animal first followed by the bacteria illness. Pneumonia is so dangerous owning to the fact that once it strikes an animal, after the customary symptoms that will follow the animal is very likely to die soon after or recover just as quick but would suffer permanent damage to the lung. As earlier stated, such a diseased animal could be the one that introduces the very stubborn disease to your herd.

Pneumonia can affect almost any grown up cow but calves are more susceptible to it owing to the fact that they are yet to have a fully developed immune system that can convincingly battle the disease and succeed.

At the initial stages there are various causes of viruses to beef cattle, from parainfluenza to enterovirus. Adenovirus, herpesvirus, rhinovirus, bovine viral diarrhea and respiratory syncytial virus, etc.

It is common knowledge that once an animal has caught the disease, it becomes an uphill task to cure them of it and even if the animal does get better, it can never be as good as new. But there is good news; there are vaccines that can protect your herd from these troublesome viruses.

Bacteria just as viruses, also have different causes but amongst them, two irksome culprits stand out: the pasteurella multocida and the mannheimia haemolytical. Again, calves and newly weaned cows are soft targets for these bacteria.

There are signs to look out for in cattle that tell that pneumonia is imminent. Often than not, a cow that has been struck by this disease might go through a phase of viral respiratory tract infection. Afterwards, when the germs have matured, the symptoms get stronger and more prominent.

Let's talk about these troublesome bacteria a bit:

Pasteurella Multocida

If you know one or two things about cattle and cattle diseases, then you should have heard of pasteurellosis otherwise known as pasteurella Multocida. It is known to affect the respiratory tract of its victims leading to bovine respiratory disease. Pasteurella Multocida doesn't just affect cows directly. The animal first has to be having its immune system weakened by a viral disease before a way can be paved for the Pasteurella Multocida to attack.

As expected, when your animals are penned together, the chance of these bacteria or any bacteria for that matter to spread at all becomes greatly increased. Pasteurella Multocida would cause your animal to catch a disease which it would inhale deep into the respiratory tract and the cow's immune system has been weakened probably as a result of stress or some other reason. It can be passed on from one animal to another through direct contact, ingestion of water or ingestion of food that has been contaminated by an affected cow.

There are signs that tell you that you might be dealing with Pasteurella Multocida and they could get real ugly sometimes. Pasteurella Multocida is associated with problems of respiratory disease that persist for a very long time. Some of the signs that tell you that you might be dealing with Pasteurella Multocida is that your animal could become depressed. They would become so unhealthily broody which should be call for serious concern. Also the willingness to eat suddenly vanishes and this is easy to spot. Cattle are animals that do more eating than any other activity. You could even say that they eat for more than half of their life so when they are surrounded by these fresh and tasty looking pasture and they don't eat, it tells that something is the problem and should be dealt with as soon as possible.

Your animal would completely lose its appetite if the problem persists. Then there become problems of lowered heads and noses and nasty nose discharge. Your animal would go into great discomfort as she would find it really painful to breath coupled with some equally painful cough. If you have allowed it to get to this stage, then it is your last chance to get help. Visit an animal specialist for recommendation or treatment because if the animal is left to it's terms, the disease becomes irreversible and ultimately leads to the death of the animal.

It is always advisable to go to a specialist before things get very serious but which ever stage your decide to visit the vet or whoever, there are certain diagnosis you are most likely to see.

- Increase bronchial sounds and wheezes
- Limited lung necrosis
- Bronchiolitis
- Thrombosis
  And others…

The stage of the disease where your animal is at before you reported the specialist would heavily determine the mode of treatment of the animal. Early everything is recommended and so early discovery of Pasteurella Multocida and quick action would prove favorable for you. One thing that would be almost constant in the treatment of Pasteurella Multocida related problems are the use of antibiotics. Antibiotics are very crucial because it would stop the progression growth of this disease.

Several antibiotics will do the trick but the most effective will be the one that works against the three gram negative bacteria that is mostly familiar with cattle respiratory problems.

It is advisable to continue the antibiotic treatment even after when you think your cow has recovered from the problem.

I will never get tired of saying that a single act of prevention is better than a hundred attempts at curing an ailing animal.

Experts say that Pasteurella Multocida and related problems are caused as a result of stress and viruses that are associated with shipping fever and so common sense says that the best way to avoid it is to relieve your animals of such stress and prevent them from viral diseases that are associated with shipping fever.

Cut down on some of the things that you think might cause stress, introduces adequate measures to control parasites and review the feed you give to your animals; consider introducing meal with more nutrition and immunize the animals early enough.

Mannheimia haemolytical

Mannheimia haemolytical also called bovine pneumonic pasteurellosis or even calf pneumonia is another infamous bacterium that is very prevalent in the life of cattle. This anomaly has caused a great number of cattle mortality over the years and is also very responsible for cattle deaths.

At the onset, your animal could be a carrier of Mannheimia haemolytical and not show a single sign. It could be caused by over stressing of cattle from transportation of herd to a different location where the cow may catch viruses' viz bovine viral diarrhea, parainflenzavirus 3 or even bovine herpesvirus. These viruses go to work on the respiratory tract of the cow, damaging the upper lining thereby paving way for the Mannheimia haemolytical to come in unhindered. When the bacterium is inhaled by the animal which becomes inevitable once it enters inside, it goes into the lower tract where it wrecks its havoc.

Even worse, when this takes place, other bacteria capitalize on this opening and cause even more harm to the respiratory tissue. Examples of such bacteria are apsteurella multocida and Actinomyces pyogenes.

There is something called the parti Mannheimia haemolytical. Experts says that it is the major cause of bovine pneumonic respiratory disease otherwise known as shipping fever. This disease should be avoided like a plague with every means necessary especially by cattle farmers because of the weight of the loss that would be incurred if it strikes a herd.

Studies have shown that shipping fever is responsible for 30 percent of the loss of cattle in the world.

There are signs that could mean that your animal has been affected by Mannheimia haemolytical which includes cough, weight loss and nasal discharge.

It does affect a whole lot of host animals such as the bos grunniens, bos indicus, bos Taurus. As earlier mentioned, the causes could be traced back to transportation of cattle and the penning together of different animals from different climate locations. Other second class viruses could also cause your cow to be affected when they attack your animal's immune system and pave way for the bacteria to go through.

Mannheimia haemolytical affects animals at any part of the world but are most prevalent in Asia and in places where rearing of goats and sheep is the order of the day.

As always it is crucial to detect any problem and most crucial to detect this one on time and take the necessary action. More than often when cows are affected by Mannheimia haemolytical they generally become depressed most of the time. They suffer great loss of weight and experience respiratory discomfort, cough and nasal discharge. In most cases, the animal dies within 48 hours of when the symptoms begin to manifest. Other signs to look out for that may indicate Mannheimia haemolytical are: dehydration, fever, fatigue, general weakness, lameness and limping.

Mannheimia haemolytical moves systematically and the animal's body which is why it should be dealt with as soon as it is detected. After it has succeeded in taking over control of the upper tract of the respiratory system, it moves on to seize that of the lower tract and then it enters the alveolar areas. At this stage it causes critical damages that would lead to pulmonary dysfunction.

In areas where cattle rearing are a major thing, Mannheimia haemolytical is a major cause of dwindling profit and losses of calves. Studies show that in North America alone, over one billion dollars loss could be traced back to Mannheimia haemolytical.

A vet or other expert should be consulted before administering any sort of treatment to your animals. Some drugs that are likely to be administered to your infected cows include: danofloxacin, marbofloxacin, oxytetracycline, tilmicosin, etc.

Like most bacteria diseases, the best treatment method would be to administer the right antibiotic to the infected animals. Examples of such antibiotics have been mentioned above.

It should be noted that there have been discussions of resistant strains of Mannheimia haemolytical which is believed to have been caused by widespread use of antibiotics. That aside, mass spread treatment of cows with antibiotics is not very advisable as it promotes transfer of antibiotic resistant genes from animals to humans.

Vaccines such as presponse SQ, pulmo-guard PH-M, pyramid 4 and other recommended ones could be administered on the orders of a vet, to immunize the herd from Mannheimia haemolytical.

Parasite control

It has been well established by now that bacteria do greatly reduce the general productivity in a beef cattle setting. But it is not just bacteria that can wreck such havoc to your finance books at the end of the day. There is also the problem of parasites; internal parasites. Parasite could even be more dangerous that bacteria problems because of its discreet nature. It becomes very difficult to notice and leaves nothing spared at its wake. Some losses that are caused by parasite would include loss of weight, reduction in milk production, slow puberty and even fertility problems.

Here's how parasite works. They find themselves a nice host and attach themselves to such host, then they feed or acquire protection or otherwise at the expense of the host. Sometimes the parasite cause enough harm to the host strong enough to kill the host. They are capable of causing devastating damages in the intestine as well as the stomach.

Cattle is a "great" host for several kinds of parasites but the most common threat to the state of a cattle's health is from internal parasites otherwise known as worms which harbor around the intestines and stomach in cattle.

To control these parasites, several measures can be taken but what you should deal with first of is to reorganize the management of the pasture on your ranch or farm. Feeding is everything in cattle rearing and so you must rely on efficient and quality pasture for good growth of your cows. However, it is through this grazing process that young cattle get exposes to all kinds of parasite larvae. One of the common internal parasites that attach itself to cows is the Ostertagia species. The Ostertagia parasite spreads when cows that are infected pass the eggs in the manure. These eggs would usually hatch within 14 days and then the larvae moves from the manure up to the grass and are eaten by the cattle.

Cows that are affected by Ostertagia usually show signs such as swelling, anemia, reduced appetite, loss in weight and malnourishment. If the symptoms are allowed to persist, they would get worse and worse and would eventually lead to death.

Prevention and control of parasites cannot be overemphasized. A cattle rearer must develop a proper and effective parasite control program to cut down on the number of worms that harbor around the stomach and intestinal region of the cow.

For there to be an effective parasite control system, you must take into cognizance certain factors; pasture control, feedlot control and animal control are such factors that should be taken into consideration.

Pasture control is critical in the controlling of parasites. It is when the larvae finds its way up the grass blades and is consumed by the animal that they get infected. The way out is to eliminate areas and conditions that are favorable to the larvae thus preventing them from accumulating.

Well calculated pasture rotation would translate to clean and safe pasture with low infective larvae which is quite what your cattle need.

Feedlot control too is crucial in minimizing parasitic growth in your herd. A dry feedlot which has undergone anthelmintic treatment could be referred to as a clean and safe lot.

In the animal themselves, adult cattle are more parasite resistant than their younger ones but it doesn't mean that they are not affected by parasites. Deworming these older cattle wouldn't be such a bad idea. If done properly, strategic deworming greatly reduces the risk of reinfection. Strategic deworming could be before introducing clean pasture or before entering dry-lot conditions.

Deworming

It it advisable to deworm light weight calves to increase their reaction to vaccines and vaccination.

There are very many recommended dewormers that are available for eliminating parasites in cattle. They may come as an injection, in oral forms or even pour-on forms. Experts recommend that they should be changed every 2 years.

Finding a good vet

Spotting a good cattle doctor isn't rocket science. Certainly you must know cattle farmers and they must have worked with several animal doctors long enough to know the good and the bad. It is always my single advice for new farmers to always seek for such information from veterans in the business.

CHAPTER 5

Harvesting

When you animals have attained a certain age, body condition and size, it becomes ready for harvest if it isn't sold away while alive.

In cattle though the maturity weight may differ for breeds and gender just like you have in humans. However some experts do say that the ideal weight for harvest should be between 800-1000 pounds and the height should be at about 5 feet 10 inches for a cow. While the bulls have their weight pegged at about 800-950 pounds and height at about 5 feet 8 inches.

It is imperative to know the frame score of your cattle before harvesting. The body condition of the cow tells the farmer the exact condition the cow is at, at a particular time in the production year. The most acceptable body condition figure I know of is around 0.20 inches of back fat. Meaning that the cattle should be harvested at a body condition of greater than 5.

How To Find A Slaughter House/Packer

Discovering a slaughter house has never been the problem but discovering one that is good is the issue. When considering a slaughter house you must take into consideration the cost of transportation, distance as your cows will be confined to a small space for a long time without food and water, if possible you should have a fair idea of their track record and know their stance on humane slaughtering which has become a law in most places.

You will most likely find enough slaughter houses that fit the description. How do you narrow it down to one that works for you? I bet their pricing will differ. Don't just go for the first good slaughter house, they might want to make a fortune off you. Compare the prices and chose the one that is most cost effective.

Getting The Meat Processed For Sale

To curb any menace that might occur it any stage during agricultural production, most governments have fashioned out a means to certify only farmers that meet the requirement and thus qualify to deal.

In America, the United States Department of Agriculture ensures that only food and other agriculture products that are safe can go into circulation. They issue out a certificate to qualifying parties as such.

It becomes even better for you to own the certificate as it gives status and recognition to businesses that possess it. Businesses however must follow certain laid down guidelines to become USDA certified.

To obtain the USDA certificate and its equivalent in other forms would usually involve an application, review and inspection.

Joining And Selling The Processed Meat To A Farm or Cooperative

The truth of the matter is that you will not make as much money as you would when you join a beef cooperative. Time will tell you that the market isn't favorable for everybody. Some spend too much money in production and marketing and the return does no justice to all their effort.

A cooperative is a collaboration with other farmers that will not only increase the returns at the end of it all but will also greatly reduce the work load. With a cooperative, your options can only grow bigger in terms of a market plan and who to sell to and where to sell.

Why does a cooperative command more selling strength than most individual owned farms? Someone once asked. I think it's a psyche thing. Most beef buyers actually trust the judgment of a group of "expert" farmers than one single farmer hence the high patronage to the sales call of a cooperative.

In a nutshell, a cooperative has it all figured out in a manner of speaking. They already have a system that works for sorting buyers and distribution of their meat.

Believe it when you hear that cooperative members are making twice the amount they made when they were solo because it's true.

CHAPTER 6

Selling Your Cattle

Other than taking your cow over to the slaughter house to get beef for sales, another method for making profit off your cattle is by selling them off 'alive'. Selling your cattle could fetch you a whole lot of money if you get it right and by that I mean that you should know the right time to sell them.

Selling during the spring

During the spring cows do require lesser feed and cost in terms of maintenance thus making it a ripe time for buyers to line and jostle to get their hands on any available nice breed of cattle. During such periods, they are willing to offer very high initial cost just to get in the mix of things. They know very well that having a cow during the summer would hike up the cost of the animals.

Another reason to sell in the spring is when you lack access to adequate pasture. Purchasing and sorting out hay and other cow feed during the period could be very cost unfriendly hence the need to sell off while you can.

Selling off cows in the winter is very likely to sell high in very cold climates as inhabitants of such area mostly have a knack for stocking up for when things get rough.

Selling during fall

You might not get as much as you get when you sell in the spring as when you sell in the fall and you might not find it as easy to sell but selling during fall is the best time there is to sell.

With winter comes a harsh and unpleasant climate condition which comes with equally tough costs of maintenance and buying of feed for your cattle. Selling them off in the fall does eliminate these problems.

You might also have very old head of cattle within your herd. Such cattle would find it tough during the winter and might not make it to the next fall alive. Selling them off before they get to experience such season in your hands means you get to make some profit off them.

Selling bulls, calves, cows. Which are the best to sell?

Generally bulls are easier to rear especially as they have better endurance to bear harsher conditions but as they get older, they become more difficult to manage as they become hotter tempered and mostly bored.

Calves are more susceptible to viruses and diseases but you do need a calf to get to a bull or a cow.

Whichever one you decide to sell should come down to situation.

Selling to your neighbors and others in your local community

Sometimes you might not need to go the extra mile to get buyers for your herd. The buyers you find either in the market or at livestock auctions are people who live in houses and some of them might just be your neighbors or people in close by communities.

It wouldn't hurt to spread the word a bit that you have some cattle for sale and even put up a sign around the house or at any other nearby place.

Selling at livestock auctions

Lately buying and selling of cattle at auctions have become more or less rampant. It is seen as a very lucrative way of earning by both buyers and sellers and as such, more people have chosen to indulge in it. The whole idea is for cattle sellers to rear their cattle to the best health possible as buyers are seeking to buy the healthiest ones they see. So while sellers are looking out to get the best price they possibly can, buyers are looking for healthy breeds as some of them look to sell them off later on.

Choosing them right type of cattle for selling purpose is essential. Buyers require high quality cows and so to get these high quality cows, you must buy them as high quality as they are young.

We have talked about some good cattle breeds in the early chapters of this book. Breeds like the Angus tend to fetch higher prices in the market than most other ones as a result of ability to produce high quality meat. A good breed though doesn't guarantee high quality. Certain benchmarks must be met to tag a particular animal as high quality such as the annual milk production rate of the cow. Cows that produce more milk are generally of higher quality than those that produce less.

Keeping cattle during the spring becomes more tedious with the whole dealing with cattle pregnancy and maintaining the calves. You might want to get help to assist you in this regard.

Whether you intend to sell just some cows or you want to sell them in their hundreds, you must do very well to prepare them for auction. To have a profitable sale, you must be conversant with the market value of the animal or animals you intend to sell so that you can have a good grasp of what yours should go for.

Know how to play with prices and also it will be smart to obtain milk from cattle even while waiting for them to be sold.

CONCLUSION

Raising beef cattle is all kinds of good and lucrative but only if you get it right.

It is quite profitable but going at it just for the money might mark the beginning of a failed business. Learn to love it and you will succeed.

Follow every laid down step and restrain from cutting corners.

It might be a long road to the finish line but it is definitely worth it.

Finally, could you please do me a favor and leave a review on Amazon if you have enjoyed this book.

Thanks and good luck in your journey,

Carson Wyatt.

www.FunHappyLives.com

www.ingramcontent.com/pod-product-compliance
Lightning Source LLC
Chambersburg PA
CBHW070108210526
45170CB00013B/789